THIS BOOK BELONGS TO:

CONTACT INFORMATION	
NAME:	
ADDRESS:	
PHONE:	

START / END DATES

_____ / _____ / _____   TO   _____ / _____ / _____

DEDICATION

This book is dedicated to all the amazing Boat Owners out there!

You are my inspiration in producing books and I'm excited to help in the planning of your boating interests around the world!

How to Use this Boat Logbook:

The purpose of this Boat Record Logbook is to keep all your various boating and maintenance activities and ideas organized in one easy to find spot. Here are some simple guidelines to follow so you can make the most of using this book:

The first "Boat Log and Record" section is for you to write out the date, weather, wind, sea conditions, and destination information so you can track all your boating adventures...

Most ideas are inspired by something we have seen. Use the "Boat Motor Maintenance" section to write down your boat make, year, motor make, model, HIN, serial number, engine hours and services completed so you can go back there to be reminded later...

The "Crew and Passenger" section is for you to write out the names of everyone on board, crew members, passengers to ensure a record of safety if needed...

And finally more pages with the "Engine Hours/Mechanic Work Needed" section is great for writing out the hours on the current engine, mechanic work necessary and pump outs of the vessel…

The "Photo" section is for you to keep a visual reminder of what your boat journey looks like. Especially helpful for selling the boat later on…...

Whether you're a first time boat owner or have been at it for a while, you will want to write everything down in this notebook to look back on and always remember your sailing time adventures.

This boat log and record planner can also be a great gift idea for boaters! Size is 8 X 10 inches, 120 pages, soft matte finish cover.

Enjoy!

BOAT LOG AND RECORD

DATE		DESTINATION	
WEATHER		FORECAST	
WIND		VISIBILITY	
SEA CONDITIONS		ETA	

TIME	COURSE	SPEED	DISTANCE	NAVIGATION NOTES	REMARKS

EVENTS /OBSERVATIONS

TIME COMPLETED		DAYS RUN	
AVERAGE SPEED		FUEL ON BOARD	
CREW & GUESTS			

CAPTAIN	

BOAT LOG AND RECORD

ENGINE HOURS	MECHANIC WORK NEEDED	PUMP OUTS

BOAT/MOTOR MAINTENANCE LOG

BOAT MAKE		MODEL			
YEAR		HIN			
MOTOR MAKE		MODEL		SERIAL #	

DATE (MM/DD/YY)	ENGINE HOURS (P/S)	SERVICE(S) COMPLETED	COMPLETED BY	WORK ORDER #

BOAT PASSENGERS LOG

NAME	DATE

BOAT CREW LOG

NAME	DATE	TIME IN	TIME OUT

ABOUT MY BOAT

MY BOAT

BOAT LOG AND RECORD

DATE		DESTINATION	
WEATHER		FORECAST	
WIND		VISIBILITY	
SEA CONDITIONS		ETA	

TIME	COURSE	SPEED	DISTANCE	NAVIGATION NOTES	REMARKS

EVENTS /OBSERVATIONS

TIME COMPLETED		DAYS RUN	
AVERAGE SPEED		FUEL ON BOARD	
CREW & GUESTS			

CAPTAIN	

BOAT LOG AND RECORD

ENGINE HOURS	MECHANIC WORK NEEDED	PUMP OUTS

BOAT/MOTOR MAINTENANCE LOG

BOAT MAKE		MODEL			
YEAR		HIN			
MOTOR MAKE		MODEL		SERIAL #	

DATE (MM/DD/YY)	ENGINE HOURS (P/S)	SERVICE(S) COMPLETED	COMPLETED BY	WORK ORDER #

BOAT PASSENGERS LOG

NAME	DATE

BOAT CREW LOG

NAME	DATE	TIME IN	TIME OUT

ABOUT MY BOAT

MY BOAT

BOAT LOG AND RECORD

DATE		DESTINATION	
WEATHER		FORECAST	
WIND		VISIBILITY	
SEA CONDITIONS		ETA	

TIME	COURSE	SPEED	DISTANCE	NAVIGATION NOTES	REMARKS

EVENTS /OBSERVATIONS

TIME COMPLETED		DAYS RUN	
AVERAGE SPEED		FUEL ON BOARD	

CREW & GUESTS	

CAPTAIN	

BOAT LOG AND RECORD

ENGINE HOURS	MECHANIC WORK NEEDED	PUMP OUTS

BOAT/MOTOR MAINTENANCE LOG

BOAT MAKE		MODEL			
YEAR		HIN			
MOTOR MAKE		MODEL		SERIAL #	

DATE (MM/DD/YY)	ENGINE HOURS (P/S)	SERVICE(S) COMPLETED	COMPLETED BY	WORK ORDER #

BOAT PASSENGERS LOG

NAME	DATE

BOAT CREW LOG

NAME	DATE	TIME IN	TIME OUT

ABOUT MY BOAT

MY BOAT

BOAT LOG AND RECORD

DATE		DESTINATION	
WEATHER		FORECAST	
WIND		VISIBILITY	
SEA CONDITIONS		ETA	

TIME	COURSE	SPEED	DISTANCE	NAVIGATION NOTES	REMARKS

EVENTS /OBSERVATIONS

TIME COMPLETED		DAYS RUN	
AVERAGE SPEED		FUEL ON BOARD	
CREW & GUESTS			

CAPTAIN	

BOAT LOG AND RECORD

ENGINE HOURS	MECHANIC WORK NEEDED	PUMP OUTS

BOAT/MOTOR MAINTENANCE LOG

BOAT MAKE		MODEL		
YEAR		HIN		
MOTOR MAKE		MODEL		SERIAL #

DATE (MM/DD/YY)	ENGINE HOURS (P/S)	SERVICE(S) COMPLETED	COMPLETED BY	WORK ORDER #

BOAT PASSENGERS LOG

NAME	DATE

BOAT CREW LOG

NAME	DATE	TIME IN	TIME OUT

ABOUT MY BOAT

MY BOAT

BOAT LOG AND RECORD

DATE		DESTINATION	
WEATHER		FORECAST	
WIND		VISIBILITY	
SEA CONDITIONS		ETA	

TIME	COURSE	SPEED	DISTANCE	NAVIGATION NOTES	REMARKS

EVENTS /OBSERVATIONS

TIME COMPLETED		DAYS RUN	
AVERAGE SPEED		FUEL ON BOARD	
CREW & GUESTS			

CAPTAIN	

BOAT LOG AND RECORD

ENGINE HOURS	MECHANIC WORK NEEDED	PUMP OUTS

BOAT/MOTOR MAINTENANCE LOG

BOAT MAKE		MODEL			
YEAR		HIN			
MOTOR MAKE		MODEL		SERIAL #	

DATE (MM/DD/YY)	ENGINE HOURS (P/S)	SERVICE(S) COMPLETED	COMPLETED BY	WORK ORDER #

BOAT PASSENGERS LOG

NAME	DATE

BOAT CREW LOG

NAME	DATE	TIME IN	TIME OUT

ABOUT MY BOAT

MY BOAT

BOAT LOG AND RECORD

DATE		DESTINATION	
WEATHER		FORECAST	
WIND		VISIBILITY	
SEA CONDITIONS		ETA	

TIME	COURSE	SPEED	DISTANCE	NAVIGATION NOTES	REMARKS

EVENTS /OBSERVATIONS

TIME COMPLETED		DAYS RUN	
AVERAGE SPEED		FUEL ON BOARD	
CREW & GUESTS			

CAPTAIN	

BOAT LOG AND RECORD

ENGINE HOURS	MECHANIC WORK NEEDED	PUMP OUTS

BOAT/MOTOR MAINTENANCE LOG

BOAT MAKE		MODEL			
YEAR		HIN			
MOTOR MAKE		MODEL		SERIAL #	

DATE (MM/DD/YY)	ENGINE HOURS (P/S)	SERVICE(S) COMPLETED	COMPLETED BY	WORK ORDER #

BOAT PASSENGERS LOG

NAME	DATE

BOAT CREW LOG

NAME	DATE	TIME IN	TIME OUT

ABOUT MY BOAT

MY BOAT

BOAT LOG AND RECORD

DATE		DESTINATION	
WEATHER		FORECAST	
WIND		VISIBILITY	
SEA CONDITIONS		ETA	

TIME	COURSE	SPEED	DISTANCE	NAVIGATION NOTES	REMARKS

EVENTS /OBSERVATIONS

TIME COMPLETED		DAYS RUN	
AVERAGE SPEED		FUEL ON BOARD	
CREW & GUESTS			
CAPTAIN			

BOAT LOG AND RECORD

ENGINE HOURS	MECHANIC WORK NEEDED	PUMP OUTS

BOAT/MOTOR MAINTENANCE LOG

BOAT MAKE		MODEL			
YEAR		HIN			
MOTOR MAKE		MODEL		SERIAL #	

DATE (MM/DD/YY)	ENGINE HOURS (P/S)	SERVICE(S) COMPLETED	COMPLETED BY	WORK ORDER #

BOAT PASSENGERS LOG

NAME	DATE

BOAT CREW LOG

NAME	DATE	TIME IN	TIME OUT

ABOUT MY BOAT

MY BOAT

BOAT LOG AND RECORD

DATE		DESTINATION	
WEATHER		FORECAST	
WIND		VISIBILITY	
SEA CONDITIONS		ETA	

TIME	COURSE	SPEED	DISTANCE	NAVIGATION NOTES	REMARKS

EVENTS /OBSERVATIONS

TIME COMPLETED		DAYS RUN	
AVERAGE SPEED		FUEL ON BOARD	
CREW & GUESTS			

CAPTAIN	

BOAT LOG AND RECORD

ENGINE HOURS	MECHANIC WORK NEEDED	PUMP OUTS

BOAT/MOTOR MAINTENANCE LOG

BOAT MAKE		MODEL			
YEAR		HIN			
MOTOR MAKE		MODEL		SERIAL #	

DATE (MM/DD/YY)	ENGINE HOURS (P/S)	SERVICE(S) COMPLETED	COMPLETED BY	WORK ORDER #

BOAT PASSENGERS LOG

NAME	DATE

BOAT CREW LOG

NAME	DATE	TIME IN	TIME OUT

ABOUT MY BOAT

MY BOAT

BOAT LOG AND RECORD

DATE		DESTINATION	
WEATHER		FORECAST	
WIND		VISIBILITY	
SEA CONDITIONS		ETA	

TIME	COURSE	SPEED	DISTANCE	NAVIGATION NOTES	REMARKS

EVENTS /OBSERVATIONS

TIME COMPLETED		DAYS RUN		
AVERAGE SPEED		FUEL ON BOARD		
CREW & GUESTS				

CAPTAIN	

BOAT LOG AND RECORD

ENGINE HOURS	MECHANIC WORK NEEDED	PUMP OUTS

BOAT/MOTOR MAINTENANCE LOG

BOAT MAKE		MODEL			
YEAR		HIN			
MOTOR MAKE		MODEL		SERIAL #	

DATE (MM/DD/YY)	ENGINE HOURS (P/S)	SERVICE(S) COMPLETED	COMPLETED BY	WORK ORDER #

BOAT PASSENGERS LOG

NAME	DATE

BOAT CREW LOG

NAME	DATE	TIME IN	TIME OUT

ABOUT MY BOAT

MY BOAT

BOAT LOG AND RECORD

DATE		DESTINATION	
WEATHER		FORECAST	
WIND		VISIBILITY	
SEA CONDITIONS		ETA	

TIME	COURSE	SPEED	DISTANCE	NAVIGATION NOTES	REMARKS

EVENTS /OBSERVATIONS

TIME COMPLETED		DAYS RUN	
AVERAGE SPEED		FUEL ON BOARD	
CREW & GUESTS			

CAPTAIN	

BOAT LOG AND RECORD

ENGINE HOURS	MECHANIC WORK NEEDED	PUMP OUTS

BOAT/MOTOR MAINTENANCE LOG

BOAT MAKE		MODEL		
YEAR		HIN		
MOTOR MAKE		MODEL		SERIAL #

DATE (MM/DD/YY)	ENGINE HOURS (P/S)	SERVICE(S) COMPLETED	COMPLETED BY	WORK ORDER #

BOAT PASSENGERS LOG

NAME	DATE

BOAT CREW LOG

NAME	DATE	TIME IN	TIME OUT

ABOUT MY BOAT

MY BOAT

BOAT LOG AND RECORD

DATE		DESTINATION	
WEATHER		FORECAST	
WIND		VISIBILITY	
SEA CONDITIONS		ETA	

TIME	COURSE	SPEED	DISTANCE	NAVIGATION NOTES	REMARKS

EVENTS /OBSERVATIONS

TIME COMPLETED		DAYS RUN	
AVERAGE SPEED		FUEL ON BOARD	
CREW & GUESTS			

CAPTAIN	

BOAT LOG AND RECORD

ENGINE HOURS	MECHANIC WORK NEEDED	PUMP OUTS

BOAT/MOTOR MAINTENANCE LOG

BOAT MAKE		MODEL			
YEAR		HIN			
MOTOR MAKE		MODEL		SERIAL #	

DATE (MM/DD/YY)	ENGINE HOURS (P/S)	SERVICE(S) COMPLETED	COMPLETED BY	WORK ORDER #

BOAT PASSENGERS LOG

NAME	DATE

BOAT CREW LOG

NAME	DATE	TIME IN	TIME OUT

ABOUT MY BOAT

MY BOAT

BOAT LOG AND RECORD

DATE		DESTINATION	
WEATHER		FORECAST	
WIND		VISIBILITY	
SEA CONDITIONS		ETA	

TIME	COURSE	SPEED	DISTANCE	NAVIGATION NOTES	REMARKS

EVENTS /OBSERVATIONS

TIME COMPLETED		DAYS RUN	
AVERAGE SPEED		FUEL ON BOARD	
CREW & GUESTS			
CAPTAIN			

BOAT LOG AND RECORD

ENGINE HOURS	MECHANIC WORK NEEDED	PUMP OUTS

BOAT/MOTOR MAINTENANCE LOG

BOAT MAKE		MODEL			
YEAR		HIN			
MOTOR MAKE		MODEL		SERIAL #	

DATE (MM/DD/YY)	ENGINE HOURS (P/S)	SERVICE(S) COMPLETED	COMPLETED BY	WORK ORDER #

BOAT PASSENGERS LOG

NAME	DATE

BOAT CREW LOG

NAME	DATE	TIME IN	TIME OUT

ABOUT MY BOAT

MY BOAT

BOAT LOG AND RECORD

DATE		DESTINATION	
WEATHER		FORECAST	
WIND		VISIBILITY	
SEA CONDITIONS		ETA	

TIME	COURSE	SPEED	DISTANCE	NAVIGATION NOTES	REMARKS

EVENTS /OBSERVATIONS

TIME COMPLETED		DAYS RUN	
AVERAGE SPEED		FUEL ON BOARD	
CREW & GUESTS			

CAPTAIN	

BOAT LOG AND RECORD

ENGINE HOURS	MECHANIC WORK NEEDED	PUMP OUTS

BOAT/MOTOR MAINTENANCE LOG

BOAT MAKE		MODEL		
YEAR		HIN		
MOTOR MAKE		MODEL		SERIAL #

DATE (MM/DD/YY)	ENGINE HOURS (P/S)	SERVICE(S) COMPLETED	COMPLETED BY	WORK ORDER #

BOAT PASSENGERS LOG

NAME	DATE

BOAT CREW LOG

NAME	DATE	TIME IN	TIME OUT

ABOUT MY BOAT

MY BOAT

BOAT LOG AND RECORD

DATE		DESTINATION	
WEATHER		FORECAST	
WIND		VISIBILITY	
SEA CONDITIONS		ETA	

TIME	COURSE	SPEED	DISTANCE	NAVIGATION NOTES	REMARKS

EVENTS /OBSERVATIONS

TIME COMPLETED		DAYS RUN	
AVERAGE SPEED		FUEL ON BOARD	
CREW & GUESTS			

CAPTAIN	

BOAT LOG AND RECORD

ENGINE HOURS	MECHANIC WORK NEEDED	PUMP OUTS

BOAT/MOTOR MAINTENANCE LOG

BOAT MAKE		MODEL			
YEAR		HIN			
MOTOR MAKE		MODEL		SERIAL #	

DATE (MM/DD/YY)	ENGINE HOURS (P/S)	SERVICE(S) COMPLETED	COMPLETED BY	WORK ORDER #

BOAT PASSENGERS LOG

NAME	DATE

BOAT CREW LOG

NAME	DATE	TIME IN	TIME OUT

ABOUT MY BOAT

MY BOAT

BOAT LOG AND RECORD

DATE		DESTINATION	
WEATHER		FORECAST	
WIND		VISIBILITY	
SEA CONDITIONS		ETA	

TIME	COURSE	SPEED	DISTANCE	NAVIGATION NOTES	REMARKS

EVENTS /OBSERVATIONS

TIME COMPLETED		DAYS RUN	
AVERAGE SPEED		FUEL ON BOARD	
CREW & GUESTS			

CAPTAIN	

BOAT LOG AND RECORD

ENGINE HOURS	MECHANIC WORK NEEDED	PUMP OUTS

BOAT/MOTOR MAINTENANCE LOG

BOAT MAKE		MODEL			
YEAR		HIN			
MOTOR MAKE		MODEL		SERIAL #	

DATE (MM/DD/YY)	ENGINE HOURS (P/S)	SERVICE(S) COMPLETED	COMPLETED BY	WORK ORDER #

BOAT PASSENGERS LOG

NAME	DATE

BOAT CREW LOG

NAME	DATE	TIME IN	TIME OUT

ABOUT MY BOAT

MY BOAT

ABOUT MY BOAT

ABOUT MY BOAT